# Great-aunt Gertrude and the handbag thief

Hannie Truijens

Illustrated by John Lobban

**Chapter 1**  Trouble for two   page 3
**Chapter 2**  The handbag thief   page 8
**Chapter 3**  Let's get him!   page 12
**Chapter 4**  Never too old to learn   page 21
**Chapter 5**  Goodbye, Great-aunt Gertrude   page 28

Nelson

**Thomas Nelson and Sons Ltd**
Nelson House  Mayfield Road
Walton-on-Thames  Surrey
KT12 5PL  UK

Text © J. C. M. Truijens 1989
Illustrations © Macmillan Education Ltd 1989
This edition: illustrations © Thomas Nelson & Sons Ltd 1992
Illustrated by John Lobban

First published by Macmillan Education Ltd 1989
ISBN 0-333-48475-4

This edition published by Thomas Nelson and Sons Ltd 1992

ISBN 0-17-400554-7
NPN 9 8 7

All rights reserved.  No part of this publication may be reproduced,
copied or transmitted, save with written permission or in accordance
with the provisions of the Copyright, Design and Patents Act 1988, or
under the terms of any licence permitting limited copying issued by the
Copyright Licensing Agency, 90 Tottenham Court Road, London W1P 9HE.

Any person who does any unauthorised act in relation to this publication
may be liable to criminal prosecution and civil claims for damages.

Printed in China

# Chapter 1: Trouble for two

Great-aunt Gertrude had come to stay with us for two months. She lives on the island where my mother was born and she had never been to visit us before.

Great-aunt Gertrude is sixty-nine years old and the nicest old lady I have ever met. Her name is Gertrude Anastasia Williamson, but she tells everybody to call her Gerry.

Great-aunt Gertrude had never lived in a big town before and she wanted to see and do everything.

One day we took Great-aunt Gertrude to the zoo. She and I had a camel ride, but my camel ate her shoe. I had to lend her my shoes to wear.

Another time we took her to the fun-fair. She drove a dodgem car and bumped into some boys who were rude to her. She also knocked down three coconuts and won a very nice watch.

When Great-aunt Gertrude had been with us for four weeks she got herself into trouble. She also got me into trouble. This is how it happened.

"I'm bored, Nick," she said to me one day. "Let's think of something really exciting to do."

We both thought about it for a long time but we couldn't think of anything really exciting.

"Let's go and see what's happening in town," said Great-aunt Gertrude. "Maybe something exciting will happen to us in town."

We told Mum where we were going.

"Look after your handbag, Gerry," said Mum, "there are some handbag thieves in town."

"Don't worry, dear," said Great-aunt Gertrude, "I know what to do with handbag thieves."

It was very busy in town. Great-aunt Gertrude bought me two packets of crisps. She could only eat one.
Then she bought me an ice-cream, even though it was raining.
Mum never buys me an ice-cream when it's raining.
When Great-aunt Gertrude paid for the ice-cream some money dropped out of her purse. I quickly picked it up for her. It was a lot of money.
I saw a man watch Great-aunt Gertrude put it back into her handbag.

# **Chapter 2:** The handbag thief

When it stopped raining we went to the park. We didn't see that the man had followed us from the shop. In the park he ran past Great-aunt Gertrude and tried to pull the handbag off her shoulder.

Great-aunt Gertrude gave a loud shout. "No you don't, you rascal!"

The thief pulled at the bag but Great-aunt Gertrude wouldn't let go. I helped her to pull, but the strap broke and the thief ran off with the bag.

I ran after the thief but he was too fast for me. When I came back to Great-aunt Gertrude she was sitting on the bench and digging into her coat pocket.

"Bad luck, Nick," she said.

"What should we do, Gerry?" I asked.

"First of all we must write a report," she said. "Do you have any paper? I have a pencil in my pocket."

I didn't have any paper but we found some leaflets on a park bench.

Great-aunt Gertrude wrote on the back of the leaflets. She wrote down the date and the time of the crime. Then she described the thief.

"He was short and thin," I said.

"He had brown eyes and a long, crooked nose," she said.

"He was wearing jeans and a black leather jacket," I said.

"And we're going to get him," said Great-aunt Gertrude.

Then Great-aunt Gertrude described her bag and wrote down what was in it. She wrote:

1 red leather purse with twenty-
   five pounds and thirty pence
1 ball of string
1 pen-knife
2 used bus tickets
3 postcards of the zoo
1 broken tennis ball.

# Chapter 3: Let's get him!

We walked to the police station to report the crime. When we were nearly there we saw a short, thin man with blue jeans and a black leather jacket come out of a shop.

"That's him, Nick," said Great-aunt Gertrude.

"He's hiding something under his jacket," said Great-aunt Gertrude. "It must be my bag."

"Let's get him," I said.

I went for the man's legs. It was a very good rugby tackle. Great-aunt Gertrude sat on his back so that he couldn't get up.

"Now we've got you, you rascal," she shouted.

The man had dropped what he had been hiding under his jacket. It wasn't a handbag. It was a parcel wrapped in paper. I think he was carrying it under his jacket to keep it dry.

"Gerry," I said, "I think we've made a mistake." I pointed to the parcel on the ground.

"Oh, oh, I think we have," said Great-aunt Gertrude when she had seen the parcel. She got off the man's back. He jumped up and turned around to look at us. He had blue eyes and a short, straight nose.

"Are you two crazy?" he shouted. He ran forward and grabbed me by the arm.

"We can explain," said Great-aunt Gertrude.

"You can explain to the police," said the man. He dragged me along.

"Let him go, you bully," said Great-aunt Gertrude, "we'll come quietly."

The man wouldn't let me go until we were inside the police station.

"They attacked me," he shouted. "This kid brought me down with a rugby tackle and this crazy old woman sat on me."

The policeman looked at Great-aunt Gertrude and asked, "Is it true?"

"Yes," said Great-aunt Gertrude, "I'm afraid it is. But we can explain."

She told him the whole story and gave him the report she had written on the leaflets.

The policeman read the report and looked at Great-aunt Gertrude. He said, "I've never met an old lady who sits on people before."

Great-aunt Gertrude turned to the man we had attacked.

"I'm sorry that I sat on you, young man," she said. "It was a case of mistaken identity. You look just like the thief from the back, and you were hiding something under your jacket. I thought it was my handbag."

The man didn't look so angry any more. "I'm sorry your handbag was stolen," he said.

Then the man shook his parcel.
It tinkled like broken glass.

"That was a present for my girlfriend," he said.

"I'm sorry about that," said Great-aunt Gertrude. "What's your name?"

"Jack Parker," said the man.

"I'm Gertrude Anastasia Williamson," said Great-aunt Gertrude, "but you can call me Gerry."

The policeman telephoned Mum.
By the time she came Great-aunt Gertrude and Jack were the best of friends.

When Mum came in Great-aunt Gertrude said, "Hello dear, this is Jack Parker. He writes detective stories for television. We thought he was a thief and we broke his girlfriend's present by mistake."

Mum looked very worried. We told her what had happened. She shook her head.

"Didn't I tell you to look out for bag thieves?" she said.

"Yes, you did dear, and you were quite right," said Great-aunt Gertrude. "I have learnt my lesson."

Great-aunt Gertrude borrowed money from Mum to give to Jack.

"You must buy another present and get your clothes cleaned," she said to him. "You can't go to your girlfriend like this."

Jack said goodbye to us and left the police station. The policeman wrote out a report.

"We'll get in touch with you if we ever find your bag," he said.

Great-aunt Gertrude never saw her bag again, but she didn't seem to mind.

# Chapter 4: Never too old to learn

The next afternoon Great-aunt Gertrude and I went to the sports centre. She spoke to the man at the desk.

"Is it just for the boy?" he asked.

"No," said Great-aunt Gertrude, "it's for both of us."

The man looked very surprised.

"Don't you think you're a bit too old for this kind of thing?"

"No," said Great-aunt Gertrude.

"All right then, you can start tomorrow at four o'clock," said the man.

Then we went to a sports shop. Great-aunt Gertrude told the saleslady what she wanted.

"Small for the boy and medium for me," she said.

The saleslady looked surprised.

"Surely you're not going to...?"

"Oh yes, I am," said Great-aunt Gertrude.

We walked out with the parcels under our arms.

"We're all set," said Great-aunt Gertrude. "Now let's go home before your Mum comes looking for us with a policeman."

Great-aunt Gertrude wouldn't tell anyone at home where we had been or what was in the parcels.

"It's a secret," she said.
Mum looked a bit cross and said,
"As long as the two of you keep out of trouble."

My big sister, Sophie, kept on asking me what was in the parcels, but I wouldn't tell her.

She called me nasty and I called her nosey. She stuck out her tongue at me and I pulled a face at her.

The next day Great-aunt Gertrude and I left the house at half past three. We told Mum we were going into town. Mum looked at us as if she didn't trust us.

"Look after your money, Gerry," she said.

"Don't worry," said Great-aunt Gertrude. "I'm only taking enough for the bus fare."

We hid our parcels under our coats and went to the sports centre.

When we got to the sports centre we went into the dressing rooms to change. I was very excited. This was something I had always wanted to do.

When we had changed we went into the hall. There were ten other children waiting for the lesson to start. They all looked at Great-aunt Gertrude and laughed. She did look rather funny.

I think my Great-aunt Gertrude is the oldest lady ever to have learnt Karate.

We started the lesson and after a while the children didn't laugh at Great-aunt Gertrude any more.
She was very good for an old lady.

"That was very good, Mrs Williamson," said the Karate teacher.

"Thank you," said Great-aunt Gertrude, "but please call me Gerry."

We were so busy learning that we didn't see Mum and Sophie in the doorway. They had found out our secret.

Mum pointed at our Karate suits.

"So that's what was in the parcels," she said.

Sophie said that I looked silly in the suit but I think she was jealous of me.

"Nick and I are learning Karate," said Great-aunt Gertrude, "so that we shall know what to do with the next handbag thief we meet in the park."

# Chapter 5: Goodbye, Great-aunt Gertrude

Soon the two months were over and it was time for Great-aunt Gertrude to go home again.

"I want to give a farewell party for my friends," said Great-aunt Gertrude. "Nick will help me with the invitations."

I helped Great-aunt Gertrude to write invitations to all the friends she had made. She invited Jack Parker and the Karate teacher. She even invited the policeman.

Mum made lots of food for the party and Sophie looked after the music. Dad cleared the living room so that we could dance.

Sophie bought a new dress for the party. Great-aunt Gertrude wouldn't show Sophie what she was going to wear.

Soon it was time for the party to begin. I was the doorman and opened the door for the visitors.

Great-aunt Gertrude came downstairs in her party dress. She was wearing her blue running shoes with red stripes and yellow laces.

"They don't go with my dress," she said, "but they are nice to dance in."

Mum smiled and Dad bowed.

"You look lovely, Gerry," he said. "May I have the first dance?"

Sophie put on the music and Dad and Great-aunt Gertrude started to dance.

First they danced a slow dance, but then Sophie put on some fast music.

"Would you like to sit down, Gerry?" asked Dad.

"No, I wouldn't," said Great-aunt Gertrude. "I like this kind of music. I'll dance with Jack Parker."

Great-aunt Gertrude and Jack Parker danced all around the room. She showed Jack how to do the dance of her island. Then Mum asked Dad to dance and soon everyone in the room was dancing.

At the end of the party Dad
made a speech and we gave Great-aunt
Gertrude a farewell present.
Everyone was feeling very sad.
I was trying not to cry.

Great-aunt Gertrude held my hand and
said, "Don't be sad, Nicholas, we'll
see each other again. Your Mum and Dad
are coming to visit me next year.
I'm sure they'll take you with them."

I looked up at Dad. "Will you take
me with you, Dad?" I asked.

"We'll see," said Dad, "we'll see."